CHEESE AFTER FUKUSHIMA

POEMS FOR A CHANGING PLANET

2009-2015

BY MARCIA SLATKIN

STEPHEN F. AUSTIN STATE UNIVERSITY PRESS

For more information:
Stephen F. Austin State University Press
P.O. Box 13007 SFA Station
Nacogdoches, Texas 75962
sfapress@sfasu.edu
www.sfasu.edu/sfapress

Book design: Jerri Bourrous
Cover design: Van Howell
Cover photograph: James Balog
Author photograph: Jennifer Wilmshurst
Distrubted by Texas A&M Consortium
www.tamupress.com

LIBRARY OF CONGRESS CATALOGING-IN-PUBLICATION DATA
Slatkin, Marcia
Cheese After Fukushima/Marcia Slatkin
ISBN: 978-1-62288-154-3

For Earth
and our continuing life here.

CONTENTS

FOREWORD: The Climate Porcupine

The earth now lives
within a climate porcupine
that changes daily.
It hugs the globe, a prickly
shawl of transparent skin
so irregularly thin
it can slip from human awareness.

I have plucked quills
from this creature's pelt,
each one key to an injured system
within its tumultuous self.
And with each plume, a poem
was penned. There were some
too sharp or sticky for me to touch –

but I offer you sixty-one.
If they are forthright, concrete,
blame the anguished ink
from earth beneath that fueled them.
And as the spears are ruthless,
their darts unyielding,
they carve plain truth.

Upheaval

Song of the Sidewalk

"Often, cracks
appear on my surface –
small breaks or humps
that scar the man-made grade
slightly. People pass with ease.

But sometimes, my pavement
heaves. I feel the crush
as tectonic plates raise
my concrete. A-framed, defiant,
I jut into air, my sides like glaciers
aslant in a rough grey sea.

It is easy, then, for beings to trip
on me, to stumble,

and lean on the very tree
whose roots have gashed
my man-poured skin
and crazed it egg-shell sharp
as it yields to the thrusting

power of growth
beneath – the force

of earth breathing."

Carbon Song

"I mingle
with my lighter cousins,
borne by winds
through which we hug
the green-blue ball below.

"As temperatures shift,
they turn to mist, and fall
as rain or dew on grass
below. But I am more hardy.
Invisible, increasing as part of air,
I'll remain, and heat the world
beneath for countless years.

"My numbers rise
as those on earth
burn oil or coal. And as I
spread, I cause huge
change. Yet I am
innocent! I never asked
for power. It's just
my way, to trap heat
that then melts ice, wrings
soil dry, and whips up
storms that can drown
life below. Now

"I and my kind invade
and thicken the sky
as would swarms of transparent
locust. And our embrace
will remain, a girdling arc
that will not fade."

Melt

"Immobile, my form
was powerfully fixed
in what they call *Greenland,*
my sheets for centuries
stacked within an ocean
cold enough to keep my ice
intact. I was content.
My massive presence
ruled the waves
and trapped excess,
a glassy girdle
cinching seas.

"Now, heat from a savage sun
attacks me. Huge chunks
of what I feel as body,
and weighing a billion tons,
shear off to drift within the sea.
Disfigured, I melt
and drown at once,
the ocean rising round
a self no longer strong enough
to tame its height. I am

"afraid. If I die,
my power dissolving
into liquid surge,
the sea will rise thirty feet.
Thawed, my wave-capped corpse
will spread, swirl past, seep through
and flood all low-lying land.

"The creatures with the fleshy
legs and chests, with hair
and anxious, beating hearts
will flee my reach.
In death,

"I will be everywhere."

Jelly Elegance

"We were scorned. 'They
have no brains,' the beings with feet
would say. 'They neither walk nor see!'

"But my efficient bells ingest, expel
and spawn, while fluid tentacles
trap the food I need. And of course
I feel! I sense my prey, and strike!
Should I desire, my awnings
swirl through bursts of spray
as I ride currents within the deep.
Besides, why rush to move
if, while afloat, we eat the fish
    you long to catch, clog the nukes
    you need to cool – and spool out
    acid waste and countless eggs?

"This much is clear. There are ever
more of us in an otherwise-emptying sea.
With big game gone, this new warmth
makes our breeding easy. And farm
waste depletes oxygen we need least.

"You with the hard skulls
and digit-rich limbs, just watch
your children wail in pain. And watch
men curse as they pick us from their nets.
Then note how we perch in comfort,
a ballet of billowing silk. How and why
all this? You cleared the space –
                                so we slid in."

The Price

2,300 Lobbyists descend on Washington, intent on
personal enrichment from the embryonic Energy Bill
NY Times, March 2009

When ants smell the siren song
of crumbs on lawns at picnic's end,
in they rush! Their patent-leather parts
gleam pleasure. Though they converge,
and with great toil drag precious loot
to joyous feasts, there's little at stake.
Earth won't shift, nor will
life change.

        But when rich men
chew raw 'Bills,' then spit
in the batter, break the bowl,
and block the flame needed
to bake them – *that's* when
earth shudders.

Pregnant with rage,
she expels huge storms
as violent birth. Her sobbing
fills watery streams
whose banks cannot contain
such grief, and flood.
Her tremors tumble towns,
while fevers cause dry ground
to crack and heave.

Whom, then, will stolen crumbs console
when "change" swallows all –
the cake, the lawn, and that
blessed safety we once felt
when earth could still embrace us?

The New Way

The sweet dots of spring!
The cherry-tinged cups that
flutter, then fall and pattern
our journey with brightness!
The ghost-white of pear blooms
that gauze the sun's light.
The small spots that hang
from a thread, like stars
in a cluster above which
leaves form. Then, the fur
and the frenzy as winds
blow and dance them.

And oh, it was late this year.
How we had waited for eyes,
for lips, the faces of buds
brimming fullness and color;
a rouging of bark tips,
a swelling of seed.
And oh, how I feared
the earth had rebelled,
and held back this greening,
the birth of new things.
Beat-stopped my heart was
while waiting for spring.

But now, dripping swelter
dogs stasis, as suddenly, winter
turns summer, and leaf buds
are shocked by the blaze
of a sun perhaps potent and vicious
through change. What can

we tell them, these infants?
What can we say? Breathe
slowly, babies. Inhale, adapt.
This is the new way.

The Responsible One

We are sitting
in a space my daughter
planted in the courtyard
at the center of a city school.

There are Japanese maple,
hydrangea – and mimosa waves
her pink bloom. I see natives –
Jack-In-The-Pulpit, Solomon's
Seal, Sweet Broom.

"We want to buy land
in some remote place," she says,
"Iceland, or Tasmania –
a distant spot where those
with nothing won't besiege
and kill for the little
we've got. I fear the
worst – sea rise, storm, drought –
where basic food and water
will be scarce. We'll get
enough so those who need
to be with us – you, dad,
others in the family –
can try to survive."

She looks at me bravely,
trying hard to smile.

"My only problem
is whom to invite:
where to draw the line."

Chinatown

They are long, grey
torpedoes lying atop
and three-high in a tank
stuffed with their flesh.
People eat inside, waiters
in white jackets, lights.

Thus packed in glass,
some gills move slightly,
slowly, old gates on rusty hinges
near their agonized ears. I burst

in, pointing. "Yes, yes, yes, yes,"
the money man cries. He leaves
the till long enough
to shoo me out, then flicks
a sudden bubbler. The window
fish jolt slightly. An eye
tries to open. A tremble,
a ripple of muscle wincing.

"Look," I say to an Asian couple
who emerge, having dined. "Look!"

"What does it matter, dear?"
says the woman, patting
my shoulder. "They'll
all be eaten anyway."

Implacable

The 2009 Climate Change Conference —
With thanks to George Monbiot

Copenhagen, the center of a tunnel
on fire, hosts diplomats trapped
by the baggage of their power.

Facing walls they detest, current
news blocks the thrust of their fists.
'Must we now be constrained?'

'We dared to invade, rape, pillage, destroy.
So, damned if we'll now fear
a paltry gas some claim
portends our doom.'

Thus these rooms seethe anger.
Like the child whose tantrums rage
against a parent's rules,
grown men clench fists and kick.
Their moves are tsunamis
that ravage their neighbors' faces.
And all seek one thing only–
to "*do more business*," but hide it.
Liberate remote frontiers; find secret
places to dump; carve obscure
hidden paths toward continued,
ever-more massive growth.

Those who so hope
won't easily be recast.

Gifts For Sale

Claws curled, glare
fierce, the eagle is defiant
beneath the plush, cut
to simulate feathers.

The llama, three feet tall, his coat
a tan and caramel blend,
has gentle eyes and velvet hooves.

Adrift in snowy fur,
the horns of the mountain-goat
bend toward his sweetly
malevolent beard.

In time, will these be the sole
remnant of creatures extinct?

Will parents who bring a child
to visit, explain – "They all

once lived, thundered through,
roamed, clattered within
the forests of the wild.
See? These look almost
like the real thing!"

The Best Stove

From "Hearth Surgery," *New Yorker*, Dec. 2009

Wood, coal, dung – the world
aches as smoke scours lung. Clean
stoves could balm three billion.

Until now, clogged tubes were private
grief. When lung-space filled, wracked frames
wheezed quietly in corners, then died.
Now, with smoke unveiled as a major threat,
we know a cook-fire's belch is dirty
as a truck's. At last, stove-builders

have the spotlight. Newly-needed,
they rub their eyes, blink, preen,
then fiddle with design.
They debate the chamber's shape,
the opening size, the thickness
of a cooking grate. They test
clay, steel, ceramic, sand, brick –
and study fire's dance; gauge
its nature; plot ways
to use and tame it.

The camp "Aprovecho,"
"I make good use of," hosts
this quest for appropriate design:
low cost, low tech.

Patient, able to show how
human disease correlates
with smoke exposure,

they've now sparked
commercial interest.
So, the race is on!
May the best stove win.

Sea-Weave

2010

At first, it seemed
a blood-blister had burst –
some crude had leaked through the Gulf,
and spread like chocolate
on a child's cheek. I thought
"rig" meant tanker now on fire,
a gash on the thigh of the coast.
It will seal, I thought. Clot and heal.

But oil warped through waves,
a great loom weaving bile and tar
as it spewed through the clean
blue sea. And someone said,
"it's not a ship. It's a *pipe* drilled miles
below the ocean's floor that broke
and gapes." Vena cava breached,
aneurysm split and the peritoneum
full of blood yet the damned vessel
spurting still, black honey of the earth's
holy center pierced, thick juice loosed
and pressured to rise, colitis
at the world's core, shitting oil
that surrounds, masks, suffocates –
even as it gathers to form a brown/blue Morse
that spells *"SOS, Change course"* –
grand idea written on water –

but in a somehow
cryptic typeface
few in power
understand.

Nigerian Blues

Spring 2010

"Sure, you slick be bad, man.
It be deep, very deep, and it seem
there be no end. But we also know
such ting. In Nigeria
we see 300 spill a year, man.
They is gas flare, poison water
everywhere, an de marsh
be destroy many time.
De companies use dem old pump station,
corroding well-head, anyting
they can for small money do.
They have rust pipe that break,
platform that crack an corrode,
so oil be oozin' everywhere,
splashin' onto marsh, forest, farm,
seepin' into drinkin' well an fishin pot.
Our net be slimy, our hut abandon,
an it is million gallon spill
from de delta's well evey year.

Man, we feed forty percent
of crude the US eat. And our folk?
We live forty year, that all.
So, why you complain? Don't ask
why BP do this to you! Ask
why you company don' fix our spill too?
Why SHELL not made to apologize to me?
'Cause I jess be Ol'Black African?
So they lie, an say muss be vandal.
Muss be sabotage. No one admit

it is jess ancient infastructure.
You gulf-gape make clear
what go on here evy day.
Old. Corrode. Broke."

Obese

Have those who mix sugar, salt
and fat in myriad batters – chips,
pastries, food processed or 'fast' –
all loaded with syrup from GMO corn,
a recipe designed to induce craving –
have they seen their victims?

Mouths full, the space between
belt and chest a-bulge, arms
thickly larded, their fragile
intentions are muted by grease.

But CEOs, investors, sellers—
their intentions are crisp, man:
Sell this recipe for hunger!

Doctors care for the obese
with a knife that misses the malady's
cynical core. There are pills to melt fat,
and some tread a mill. Still, nearly
two-thirds are overfilled here,
as the system rolls a coaster
of despair.

Bus Rapid Transit

Bogota, Jakarta, Mexico City,
Cape Town, all have made aortas

out of five inner lanes
on their wide boulevards. New,
they have no plaque. Thus millions
flow quickly in buses on these "tracks."
There are periodic stations
where tickets are sold, and shuttles
carry those living far away
to a central arterial branch. This system

moves more people per mile/ hour
than do major US subways,
and costs 30 times less to build /
maintain. New engines pollute
minimally. The down-side?

The annoyance of those wedded
to a breezy, unsustainable freedom:
the gas–eating car. But see how
high tolls here scrub vascular walls
to keep masses moving.

Bus or be out of tune! It's the price
of constant baby booms, the easiest
way for blood to move, the newest
way to groove!

India's Need

"I think we should stage a passion play
starring Mr. Monsanto, who sows monoculture
with plastic seeds that need mega-water, chem-
fertilizer, and *Roundup* enough to kill competition.
This monster has reigned for forty years.

"In my home, thin men in hot spaces
were bribed to grow sugar cane – too great
a guzzler for our arid places. The dearth
was siphoned and pumped from aquifers below.
Only an anti-Christ could have planned
this feat, then spread the scourge of CO_2
to heat and change the wind's wild habits.
As gusts from ocean die, we stand here, barefoot,
praying for rain. *Sweet monsoon, do not fail us!*

"Our Gangetic Plains, once rich in millet,
a small seed that drank slowly,
is now the capital of hunger. Yet the thin,
weak men still bow before Belzebub,
whose glossy ads spew bloated power
far and wide. When, then,

"will You, great passion hero of old,
again descend? Since resurrection,
we have seen You rarely. Even crucified,
You seemed weak, eyes closed to a world
which can only recover if our enemies
are slain. And if the spikes are deep,
the years of torpor encrusted? Then I fear

"it is *we* who must claim what is ours –
the right to farm our own real seed
so we can heal."

Titanium Heart

Climate Crisis Coalition News Roundup

"My metal precisely turned,
my minute welds intact, I will work
36000 km above the earth.

"My government will spend billions
as my long robotic arms
position panels to drink in sun—
more available up there.

"It will feel lovely
and clear beyond the earth's
strong pull. I will have
all time and space. No clouds
will block strong rays I collect,
then send to Tokyo.
Within your lifetime, it is said
I will beam down power enough
to supply five-hundred thousand
homes a year. Although

"I am quiet now, not yet
assembled, much of me still
lying in a box – my titanium heart
feels so charged with mission

"it is hard to keep
the parts of my hands
resting quietly by my sides."

Thirty-Five Years After

The Anti-Nuke Activist speaks

"When I first fought, the early 70s,
before both Chernobyl
and Three Mile, it seemed,
beside grim danger,
a Rube Goldberg cartoon
for boiling water. Weren't there
cheaper down-home ways?

"Beside toxic waste
and mining spills,
our Shoreham nuke
was badly made, the concrete
spongy, and no escape
along the island's length.
But I never nightmared
a harem of nukes, a coven,
a nest of vipers resting quietly
in their quarters till smashed
by a wall of water, some then
heating critically, belching toxicity,
and failing.

"Hi-tech vets, asked to make bombs
in the 40s and 50s, learned to concentrate
capital for maximal growth and gain.

"And so these hulks
were set in place. In Fukushima now,
damaged beyond hope of containment
or repair, they spew illness,
disbelief, despair."

The Whale Spirit Guide Speaks

> "Smashed by tsunami, a coastal town
> ponders how it will carry on."
> *Intl Herald Tribune*, 2011

"I watched! They grew rice, grain, greens,
bred poultry, ate fish; they could import corn,
seeds, beans, even buy beef.
But whale-meat was an obsession
for these slight people clearly aroused
by girth and length. Now flattened,
their houses wanton shards,
these towns in past felt passion
for whale meat, and would
plague the seas with their stalking.

"What else, then, could I do?
Since biblical times, Leviathan
was dear to me. I was with
Jonah, soothing my charge.
As spirit-guide of great water-beasts,
I fashioned all my power this time
into a hugely-towering tail.
Striking the waves, it could make seas
rise and move with thunderous swell
as though the plates beneath
had erupted, split and heaved.
Should I have done less? Do you think
I would allow extinction? The earth

"is overrun by this puny Sapien species
with the feverish mind. And everywhere,
I see willful destruction. I swear,

"those towns now gone
will not again
kill my whale."

The Artist's Eye

Despite strain, bitter pain
in every scene, and massed troops
entering into war, Matt Brady
composed shots coolly,
sight guiding unflinching mind.

The aesthetic of disorder is not new.
Pollack dribbled years ago, and we have
monuments to misery by Salgado.
But every day now brings dismemberment,
grotesque fragmentation, flesh blown away.

During war, terror or carbon-aided death,
you can sometimes glimpse a scene
partially intact – perhaps a staircase,
or the crazed sag of cracked walls.
The outer hole then becomes a frame
to encase chaos. Or, if a diagonal
recedes toward a series of textured shapes—
wood, brick, sinew or bone – the gaze
leaps, despite the heart's recoil.

In the case of bomb, fire, quake
or flood, structure is less evident.
One finds rubble, or a mess of splinter
leading nowhere. Then, only repeated
angle and color twirl the optic nerve,
attempting massage.

So, despite sadness or dismay,
the artist's eye rages for pattern,
rhythm, beauty – any beauty
anywhere –

and finds it.

Cheese after Fukushima

If I were young, my ovaries
prodding possibility, squirming
newness still in my future,
I might stop. Wind and rain
bring rads to grass, unknowing
ruminants munch, and the rest
is amplification.

"Then buy skim, packed before
the Japanese release – enough
for a lifetime – and mix your ration
daily," says the health 'umai.'

But I'd so mourn lessened
pleasure: that thick milk-magic
that lets enzymes weave
such wildly unctuous tastes
undreamed.

And I wonder about farmers –
or the goats themselves,
the woolly sheep, the cows
with bursting teats, unaware
of danger lurking in a grass
that still looks green.

Bathed in sun, brushed
by wind, can they say
whether it all paid off?

Small Green Stones

I sing of bees lost in skies suddenly
trackless; of white bat noses
signaling death by the millions
and leaving high caves empty,
resonating silence. Headlines blare
about some random theft even as,
quite unnoticed, extinction rends holes
in the intricate ladder of beings,
and destroys the web of life
on earth. This year

on the limestone path leading
toward our land on the Clain, (where
in earlier years we ate wondrous fruit—
their moist seeded centers brimming joy)
figs now are small green stones for lack
of rain. I see how climate change
might manifest in Poitiers, France.
We don't yet suffer violent storms,
winds that rip and tear, floods that carry
home and life away; we don't so far
have flames that roar and scorch, or
the cracked, hapless soil of deep despair,

but rather it seems a subtle
drying, a shrinking,
a hardened loss of bounty,
until the memory of juicy bliss
scratches the tissue of the brain,
and broils it with an inner flame
there is no moisture now to douse.

Attachment

We share them the way kids
traded baseball cards in the 60s –
eagerly opening attachments –
but with pure intent – not to amass,
to boast of the biggest stack or the best
batters, but only for beauty's sake:

see spots on the back of the emerald
frog, his eye luminous, one translucent
arm grabbing an acorn, fingers as eager
as ours to grasp? Or the giraffe neck
entwined with and nuzzling its young?
Look at fold within fold on the ample
rhino rump; or the blue-green
gecko, crouching, limbs about
to spring, mouth half-open,
its shiny skin a bag of sky or sea,
its fingers flexed. I don't want

to lecture. You know what I'm saying.
I save images sent me by friends
in a file entitled "possibly
endangered." In that way,
these creatures remain
available to sight
even if someday
extinct – at least until
this hard drive fails.

OBGYN Credo

"To save time,
we induce them.
None of that wavering,
no hands held, one size
fits all. Pitocin,
epidural, legs spread,
the crowned head, then cut
catch clamp stitch – done!

If we sense distress, Cesareans
are easy, afford free weekends,
and whole-night sleep. You know,
it pays to plan ahead.

It's a lie, that death rate USA
is higher than EU, where barbaric
doulas chant their voodoo prayers.
Glad that we've put an end
to that homebirth trend. "Low-risk"
deliveries simply don't exist. We know
pregnancy always hides catastrophe
to be prevented. So we've tried to
outlaw midwifery in the US.

And if it's freedom you're crying for –
well, sweetie, suicide, as you well know,
is also illegal."

Potions

"In the veldt, and trekking
toward the buzz,
I found her, still asleep
and bleeding, her face a field
of splintered bone. The blade
had snapped her horns like twig,
striking this way, that.
All I could do was
water her when she woke,
and phone for transport.

"Some think rhino flakes
gather to a golden crown
from which flows health,
power, desire. Beetle paste also,
and monkey scrotal mash.

"So, although science finds
the curved spears useful
only to the animal itself,
all else fiction, in China
and Vietnam, ancient myth
holds horn more dear than gold.

"Ah, yes. We understand this quest.
Humans fear impotence.
Illness. Death."

Loss

Farm spray? Neonics?
Maybe twisting magnetic energy
that cause signal shifts? But this new
collapse theory seems saddest,

for who can wrench us
from convenient speech?
If cell phones cause disarray,
the sweet air, once a guide,
becomes a hostile, alien place.
Golden coats will harden
as they drop from sky,
shrink, and curl toward death.

And what of the blossoms
un-messaged: tree-weave
gone, binding ragged,
instructions incomplete,
and no pollination
toward swelling. And what

of the adults who will rarely –
or perhaps never again
taste the luscious softness
they so loved, all that red/
green/ golden pulp
drenched sweet.

How they will mourn
as their poor children,
oblivious to things
named *apple, plum, peach,*
just poke and text
text and tweet,
tweet and speak.

Aged Brigade

Japan, July, 2011

"Time tick
like bomb in my head.
In past they refuse my help.
They are wrong, and now
they pay. But world, whole
earth also will pay.

"I was lead in robotics.
We make metal robot –
can walk two legs, dance,
even play violin, Suzuki book I.

"When I see Diiechi,
I feel danger lick, like cat
wash paw. Only robot can be
safe inside, cleaning, fixing.
I beg they order fleet
not hurt by rads.

"We even build prototype,
name "Mooty," who can
climb rubble like antelope,
and radiation not harm.

"'No,' say Tokyo Electric.
'It is unnecessary. If people
see robot, they feel fear,
think possibility of accident.'
So instead, company create
'safety myth': advertise, bright page
in book, tourist place with pregnant

women guide, so people think,
if mother there, it is sure okay.

"And so, after tsunami,
when rad increase, Tokyo Electric
can nothing do. They send water
on police truck, to spray.
They send helicopter, fly over
buildings, to spit and spew.
But is just show for public,
to say, 'we care, we work for you.'
Finally, Japan must buy water
pump from China, robot
from the USA. Big shame.

"And now? I am old. Wife
die, children go from home.
Night, I wake to pee many
time. Hair stop it push through
head. I tire. And yet, I want
to try. It will take ten year
to clear the three sick plant.
From where they workers find?

"This time, maybe they not
refuse my help. I create
the AGED BRIGADE,
those who enjoy make thing good.
Reproduce no longer
our goal, and cancer
from exposure grow slowly.
So we wait for cool time.
We repair, clean, save lives.

"People say, ah, 'suicide
brigade.' But is not true.
I want just to stop bomb tick
in chest, to make shame
leave, for self-protect.
Then maybe Japan
be back on list of place
whole world again
can trust, respect."

Patience Please, Patents...

The Inventors Lament

"Our polished plans jostle
for the best place in line.
They are both balloons
emanating from our skulls,
and a series of formulae on screens
or finger-greased sheets.

"But the US patent office is a starving
cat slithering on an empty belly.
With funding cut, it subsists on a third
the calories such beasts should eat.
It's overworked staff can't consider
the dreams that crowd the counter.

"Desperate, our inventions themselves
come to life. Images rise and float
six feet over the desks. In color 3-d
they gyrate, they revolve.

"Workers glance up. Look!
A siphon for capturing heat
below volcanoes in their quiescent
but calorically enhanced state!
There's a machine to harness
wave activity, not only during
tsunamis, but whenever winds rage.
There are designs for rooftop gardens,
and solar collectors thin as flower crepe,
able to suck rays even as roads are paved.
There's a balloon–powered internet,
where blimps, drones, and cables make

a global network. There's solar spray paint
that sips sun on cloudy days.

   "And think of Sahara, Sonoran, Mohave,
   Taklimakan, Syrian, Kalahari, Atacama,
   Patagonia, Gobi, Great Victoria -

"all deserts growing constantly – the mind
reels at possibilities, passionate kisses
from the lips of the great Apollo.
Of course, storage abounds
in rainbow colors, shapes, designs.
And there might even be a way
to detoxify and store nuclear waste.

"The images shimmer above desks
as workers stare at the spectacle.
Ideas shove as they beg for the right
to a pulse –'please, just a simple heart
and lung, so we can live.' But see the line?
And they grant fewer patents per year now.
Workers who retire aren't replaced.
The young are excessed.

"So, if lucky, our proposals
will fly to China,
where the patent office
is a sleek, hungry cat, its muscles
aquiver, its pink lips
hiding sharp incisors,
its jaw lined with massive
molars, which seem
ready
      and eager
            to grind.

Future Tense

My niece, who ran marathons
in youth, sends photos
of her pregnant belly,
a four - month bulge no bigger
than the moon's new crest.

The sonogram swirls
with legs already used to kicking.

Will those muscular thighs
carry him far from flood and drought,
from twisters whirling through?
Can he flee flame and smoke
before they consume?

Will he find the peace
his mother found – a place
to plant fleet foot
as torso moves, mind
decides, hands create
and heart expands?

Or, by then
will there be ceaseless
destruction, fear,
and rushed rebuilding,

as 'change,' set in motion
like a time-bomb lit,
does what it must.

Paternal Acceptance —

Our solar system speaks…

"we feel relief as orbiting junk hurtles by…"
Intl Herald Tribune, 2011

"I don't mind, really.
There is so much of me to fill.
If I had a precise aesthetic
or were easily offended,
I would hate the debris
they heave. 'Only my nine,
and the moons circling each,' I'd say.

"But absent nuclear weapons,
I delight in the variety. I learn
human terms as they release new
pieces of clutter. Since Sputnik #1,
half-million lumps of detritus

"dumped. Luckily, I am so big
these cause me little pain –
less than a pebble in your shoe,
a splinter, dust in your eye.
I shake myself as would a wet dog
drying, and go about my life.

"Indeed, I watch their antics as a parent
views a child's first drawings,
the crayon clumsily grasped between
those chubby fingers that then wipe
snot from a nose, or suck
a lingering sweetness left
from earlier lunch.

"And like a good father,
I warn them not to fight …"

Patriotic Questions

July 4

On this day, men sit in a line,
heads back, hardy geese
set for foie gras stuffing.

Each will gulp sausage
deeply. Gullets wide,
pork dogs are shoved in
whole, each a virgin
untorn by teeth.

What juice will be needed
to process this assault?
Why does the fete entail
mounds of meat? What if
such excess causes disease?
And how about the livestock?
How much corn soy water
hormone meds farted-methane
for their rearing? Finally,

does the lust stoking
this contest, all that wild
joy and juice, mirror
our historical gift
for swallowing land abroad –
occupying, despoiling,
and ingesting entire?

Hope

The Center for Biological Diversity
prompts the US Fish and Wildlife Service
to review Endangered Species Status
for 757 species, 2011

One can imagine them
like petals of peonies
unfolding, each species
raising eyes to a sky
that will be kinder, perhaps,
when they're inscribed
for possible survival –
26 birds, 31 mammals, 67 fish
13 reptiles, 42 amphibians, 197 plants
381 invertebrates. Their curves

differ from ours, parts unlike,
but as the Buddhists say,
all sentient beings. They have
names like Pacific Walrus,
Mexican Grey Wolf, Blue-
footed Booby, and that
New England Cottontail
found in books for children.
Some are colorful, like scarlet
Hawiian honeycreeper,
or Miami blue butterfly.
There are 32 pacific mollusks.
Even Noah didn't know them all.

You can imagine their hearts
beating with relief, flesh
more peacefully settled
around the shape each takes,

circulation freely flowing toward
hope. You can imagine that diversity
thronging, an all-species parade
as they hold hands and dance. "Nearer
to protection," they'll assure
one another, skins brushing gently.
"Not there yet, but those
beings at CBD –

     at least they hear us."

Menopaused

"I am a woman newly forced
into change. My hormones
blocked, I suffer chills,
hot flashes, sweating.
My sex parts dry
as my deserts expand.

"These mood swings, dousing
tears and shaking
make my rivers swell and flood,
my seas rise. My body seems
an alien frame which beings
with power slice, chew up,
then spit like gum, or roll
like dice for gain.

"Strange that, despite their abuse,
they long to huddle in my womb.
But when no longer able to bathe
in the vanished warmth
of amniotic wet, perhaps
then they'll note with rue
how they'd been cared for
by and through me – daily."

Barcelona

In Barcelona's Rambla de Raval,
we watch street drama from our
balcony, and note that
even the local drug dealer
puts cans into the can bin,
plastics with plastic. He shows me
how to slide paper into the paper slot.
And the glass? Perhaps he enjoys
the clash of breaking, as bottles clatter
and smash down the proper chute.

Between the black capsules
which he hides in boxes
behind the wheels of parked cars;
between the cell phone frenzy
and the parade of young men
who pass ten euro notes into
and then shake his hand before
the pill is granted; between arguments
about territory and domain, about
his right to deal here, this man
of 35, his shirts cleanly washed each day,
his pants baggy but somehow neat,

this man recycles faithfully –
even the compost
into the compost bin:
even that.

On "The Beach" Again

We bring a friend
to our garden on the Clain
in Poitiers, France. We grow
zucchini, the potatoes forge
subterranean trenches, tomato vines
sag beneath fat fruit, lettuce frills
to fullness, cabbage leaves curl
while magenta beets lump the land.

        There is no Monsanto
to spread death on our silt-rich soul,
no nearby spray brought by wind
to our crops, no enrichment save fish
dung, guano, and the river's rich spill.
This is why we are here –
we grow our own good food
in this blessed moment of safety
before Poitiers is also tainted.
Our friend, whose basket
we have filled, takes our picture.
"You two look happy," she says.

I study our goofy grins,
70 but still 30 somewhere deep,
and it is true. We are as happy
as people can be despite news of
famine, war, drought, flood,
fire, bombs of terror, corporations
ruling all, and the hunch that this
is the best it will ever again be,
as we live on the tumbling sand
of the archetypal "beach,"

though our descent
will surely be slower,
more violent, more complex.

By The Pound

It is as if a child were to ignore
the presence of his mother – the food
she provides, the shelter,
the nurturance and protection –
not to mention any physical beauty
she might have – luminous eyes,
glossy hair, pleasing softness –

all invisible, she valued as a thing
to be sold by the pound, or bits
collected, chewed, swallowed raw
till the whole no longer functioned,
was invisible as a living entity,
but was seen as a mine to be pillaged,
blood siphoned, heart
and kidneys harvested,

all to be converted
    to cash: the only
            meaningful green.

Albatross in the Midway Atoll

When photographed,
the slit reveals plastic gleam,
cut or broken – orange, green,
blue, the ubiquitous grey
of a billion bottle bits,
or the black of cap-shards:
slivers of human convenience
or distraction, thrown to a landfill,
then tossed into seas.

Outside, and atop its stuffed belly,
a flurry of curled feathers ruffle
round a head leading toward
a beak more curved and elegant
than a Greek vase. The sunken eye
is shut to a world it wrongly trusted.
This chick was fed what its mom
thought food, but instead was

garbage, litter of a world
choked beneath waste.

Yes. Our own kind,
unable to discern
what might not nourish,
also trusts.

Coleridge Revisited

It is an itch untamed,
a sob that grows,
the sort of bloat that makes
a putrid can explode —

and then, as Coleridge did,
I seek and find the one
on whom to vomit woe.

Tongue unleashed, I blurt crude lists
of ills earth bore and now returns –
in heat, in flood, or the smoke-drenched
burn of a million trees.

Eyes glazed, no doubt
enmeshed in pain
that sears each wary,
troubled heart,

most really
lack the time
or space
to care.

Plastic Elixir

A young girl's song

"Blood came in 4th grade –
a dark brown blotch
on my underwear
that I didn't understand.
I'd heard about birth,
but no one said much
about breasts that swell,
or the ache down there,
that makes me rub, slip
fingers in, touch. In school,

"the big boys buzz
like flies near cake
my mother bakes.
Their hands find folds,
and thrust, until I feel
big spurts of juice, waves
that pulse, balloons
that burst and leave me limp
but wanting more. I watch

"TV –girl's parted lips,
swinging hips, darting tongues.
My teacher says what I feel
isn't 'real' – it's from some stuff
plastic bottles release.

"But this blood sure is real,
as are these nipples I rub
until they point. Real too,
is the fact that I hate

this class, can't stand to hear
what teachers say,
'cause all I want
is that boy's big thing,
that hard-ass pound
and that watery rush –
that weight, that
sweetness,
that joy."

Digital Fix

The new digital globe
gives the illusion of mastery.
We can project our home
in its entirety, parameters accurately
drawn, our hands controlling shape
and noting shifts. See how
points drift from tan to orange,
then rust, and brown in spots where
drought sucks life, or fires blaze?

I remember Chaplin playing Hitler,
twirling the world in a smug
ballet till the bubble pops.

But with us, living the change,
watching oceans swell, seeing real
drought fire storm,
   the ending will last a century,
   a protracted cacophony of disaster
   as technicians fiddle with keys, stare
   at screen, and at times hit "delete"—

maybe now to rid the map
of those pesky Pacific Islands
still singing (perhaps too loudly)
under the sea.

Plan

Jokes rarely imprint. Heard or seen,
a ripple bows my lips and makes
my cheeks rise briefly. But when

I was twenty, a cartoon
marked my soul. Two
prisoners, shackled to a stone cell wall,
ragged, stringy limbs and neck in irons,
yet were able to move their lips.
Eyes darting toward his cell mate,
"Now here's my plan," one said.

No other image so hit home
until this year when, during floods
in the drowned mid-west, a woman,
one gnarled hand clasping bathrobe shut,
the other grasping rail, stood
on her porch. Water had risen
to the second step when a polar bear,
on a lone ice shelf, floated
toward her house.

              The bear looked up.
Their eyes then met
in what must have been
a wry acknowledgement
of all we face
on this sad sphere.

If either spoke of a plan,
                  I didn't hear it.

Virtuality

A baseball player loves a woman
met on line. He texts and tweets,
till grapevines afar cheer the affair.
When news of her death sets him careening,
his fans mourn too. Later, he learns

both she and the death
were pranks by mischievous friends –
mere clicks in virtual space.
Did she ever exist as flesh?
Did he know? Was it a ploy
to gain press? Was his anguish real
or not, as she breathed pixels only?

So, when people are told
of danger we face,
as our only home
is degraded by a gas
we create while burning,
do they think the message
merely virtual, a story invented
by misanthropes hostile to happiness?
Or perhaps it requires an imaginative leap
that addicts find difficult to make?

                        Have we
sucked the globe itself of substance?
This earth that I dig in and rub
through my fingers – sand, silt, loam, clay –
is this all less real than images
manufactured on line? Will
electronics, now merely distracting,
ultimately rob our awareness

of the here-now depth
through which we move?
Will we lose track
of smell sound heft?

Is there no way back?

Being Here

Homer had Achilles
teach Odysseus the primacy
of being. "I'd rather live
a servant in the house of a tyrant
on earth, then be king
over the richest realm of the dead,"
ghost Achilles said. How to
remember this despite
gashes in the fabric of hours,
the shredding of intentions,
the looks returned devoid
of the empathy we sent.

A friend writes an e mail.
"Assignment," he says.
"On the in-breath through your nose,
think 'even this.' And when you exhale
with your open mouth, whisper:
'is enough.' Do this whenever
you can – during anger or pain,
boredom or fear.

"It will help
keep you clear."

Cheer-Casters

Hosts on the weather channel preen now:
They have the nation's full attention.
As they present shredded cities, they stay
upbeat, even jubilant as they point
to heaps of home-and-tree interwoven.

Strange that "climate change"
(as concept or reality)
is rarely mentioned. But the name
of each storm is indelibly inscribed
in the psyche of the afflicted.

Does it not seem that asteroid disasters
are alluded to more often now?
And is this devastating possibility
whipped to a froth of creamed delight
atop a cake of horrors? Is it fed
to an audience eager for racy excitement?
Perhaps complete devastation
for which we have no responsibility
is easier to accept
than slow disintegration
which we, with sacrifice,
could ameliorate, prevent.

And then there are those
who point to the speck
in the sky with a climate
perhaps similar to ours.
Should we move right in?
Should we ruin that one too?

"But," most say sadly,
"it does seem pretty far away."

The Realist

My nephew, brilliant in youth
as an organizer of charities
mitigating misfortune, now monitors

the effectiveness and honesty
of groups collecting funds post-disaster.

"No," I said. "Work instead
to *prevent* problems. Work
to slow the CO2 bloom, to stem
Monsanto GMOs, to stop
Fed subsidies of gas, oil, coal,
to promote widespread composting,
zero waste, all good alternatives!"

"But such advocacy needs willing
legislators, many of whom
suck the teat of corporate donors," he says.
"They are implacable. One would need
to alter election funding,
and rid the US of 'Citizen's United,'

all unlikely. And so we must at least
assuage the inevitable loss and pain
that comes with climate change."

Defeated, I donate.

Lourdes Under Water

Song of the Sanctuary

"God has always aided,
as the faithful pay to pray here.

"But my winding friend the Gave de Pau,
a docile presence clinging to my sides,
was pelted by storms till it bubbled; surged.
Banks yielded, and my grotto flooded,
a place of holy solace to the sick.

"Six million pilgrims left. Now my
eleven immersion pools, my crypt,
the basiliqua, all chapels are closed.
Will prayer now heal *me*?
Will the faithful give enough for *my cure*?
Those pilgrims wrenched from hotels
as the river rose, the grotto filled –
will they donate still?

"There have been sixty eight miracles
wrought here. Is this flooding sent
by Divine anger? Last autumn also
my grotto was attacked by water.
There is more snow in the Pyrenees.
Has that climate illness killed me too?

                    "Bernadette, you who saw
eighteen visions and the Virgin alive in this place,
what should I do? What of the torch-light
processions that wound through me, kindling
my power? Without force of the faithful,
I am nothing. Is my grotto itself

as liable to malady as those it cures?
Help me, Lord, to care for your creation.
Bring me wholeness, a living place
through which you continue to sing."

Rainforest Plea

"You smash, cut us down or up
to burn, build, or clear for crops
like 'palm' that bring in easy cash.
You've shrunk our native
habitat. Many creatures die. And yet

"we are earth's lungs. It is our job
to release the air you humans need,
then gulp the causes of climate disease.
What's more, we form communities.
Our roots can signal stealthily.
We lend food to neighboring trees
in need, and nurse our ill. Of course

"we sprout from seed. You see us
swell beneath our parents, green shoots
cribbed by curving roots. But you –
you thwart our growth! No! Sow,
set saplings into beds, then water
                              till we spread.

"And stop the cutting!! Grasp this truth:
we are the core, at the threshold of Earth's heart.
Your abode is being harmed! All your systems
are at risk. And we trees cannot help if gone.

"Embrace us as healers. Encouraged
to grow, we'd hold moisture in,
we'd shade warm soil, we'd gulp
harmful gas, and, abundant again,
potent leaves might restore
                    your mortally wounded home."

Our Hippo

"Massive, rotund,
the hippo of systems,
I eat coin, paper, land,
promise, dream. Always

"hungry, I am petted to skin-
shine by devoted hands. I offer
multiplication, amplification,
infinite diversity and growth.
And so they compete to feed me
at amazing rates. I alone ingest
two earth's-worth of oil, coal,
gas, wood, electronic magic,
money without backing, *yearly* –
anything to stuff my churning gut,
because I do so ravenously *need*.
Some fools try rope to reign me,
lock my lips, but I bite through.

"It's really an incredible plan –
the expandable 'in box,' my gain-rate
minutely calculated, and the inevitable
mountain of waste. Know, though,
that mine is less predictable than other
system's shit – more potent, often toxic
in secret, silent ways. But my gratified

"satiety generates wildly-rich flesh, fold
upon folds which, when cut into
succulent strips, shimmer and gleam.
Braised, they sizzle with a dark, smoky
flavor which the cognoscenti often indulge in,
climbers rave about, and those sadly
without access, *desperately crave*."

Fire's Confession

An Apology

"I flit, I dodge, I flare, a Mobius
aglow. I burrow the lattice of roots,
launch embers that spark miles away,
hit tree crowns, ski sky,

"and my siblings all aid me. Air
brushes me russet, burnishes,
fluffs me, swirls my gold reach.
Storms split and spark me,
hurl bombs that dance
as earth feeds me wood
dry as bone crunched by beetles,
grass rusty with drought.

"Men with homes on the margins
of wildland know well
that they've entered my kingdom
and might be my food.
Those firemen, children in helmets,
couldn't match my madness. They were
gone in an in-spire of my toxic breath.

"I suck, I flash, I swallow my path,
leaving little but fine-blown
brown ash. And I don't even
sense what I eat. I can't taste
or smell it, can't note or think,
for my teeth and my gullet
are caught in a frenzy of capture
which I can't prevent. I gulp,
unseeing. In gorging,
please know that I feel
no glee…"

Their Right

Of course one can't approach those
who converse. Ear phones themselves
create distance, even
if linked to air only.

But often those seemingly
at rest also raise their arms to protect
from the poison of petition.
Their polite smiles mean
"no thanks," as if offered
a product – a candy, a coffee,
a mint – instead of clean water,
less carbon, life.

              The citizens
of Oran were also reluctant
to admit the presence of plague.
Strict isolation was hard to accept.
Even when bleeding rats
crawled to streets and died?
Even when friends revealed
buboes that gushed pus? Yes.

"We want our freedom,"
they'd say. "This is our only chance
to live. We won't be controlled
by your bogus notions.
Climate change, you say? Maybe
the sun feels hotter in some places
on some days. Just…. leave us alone!
Go away!"

Native Sweat–Lodge

What I felt

I

You crawl in, not knowing
those beside you, or who
will remain in this dark space
to embrace you with chanting.
What hand will pass a ladle of cool

to slake your desire? What fears
will you hear, and then yourself speak
in this smoldering place? These rocks
trade heat for secrets, their faults
absorptive, healing. Patient,
they welcome fervor. Glowing,
they listen and wait.

II

Drops of sweat from streams between breasts
are strewn on rock as a gift, and earth
hisses her thanks. Stones cede heat
as steam. Clouds billow and rise, while
your breathing recedes to some innermost
chest, its depth so small you can't feel
what's exchanged, what is lost or gained.

Heat creeps in to loosen old glue,
as fused bones are transmuted to soup.
You think you will faint, but others
chant praise, so instead you quietly
hum without breathing. Your skin

is a wetland flooded by juice. Who knew
you had this much to give?

Your hands glide your surface, slippery
as rock under tide, bathed-skin of a self
now an infant adrift in earth's torrid womb.
And you are being rid
                              of all that is worn
within you, all that is old and tired.
And you feel reborn.

                    III

It's so simple anyone might do it.

After three rounds of healing prayer
and dripping purge, you emerge
to December air, to bald trees
that are clean as you, your body's steam
a mist that heats the December sky.
You walk amid a clump of trees,
sweet loam beneath your naked feet.
Anyone might sense it.

Your spine goes slack.
You snuggle in between dry leaves–
the brittle oak, the sharp-toothed beech
that now feel soft and welcoming.
Hovering between awareness and sleep,
your heartbeat slows, thoughts unwind,
your thin breath laps your reeling mind,
the soft stars swim pale solstice skies,

earth's pulse beats through life-drenched things –
anyone might feel it.

Then, eyes closed, the sweating stops.
Your skin, now dry, can feel the cold.
You turn; your gaze records this place.
A tipi fire has warmed the space.
And while you dress (as all might come
to sense feel know), your every breath
is praise.

Courtesy of Koch

2014

The hopeful post-Sandy TV show
pushed "remediation," a fixing
and living with, as with an illness
the men in white coats call

"idiopathic" as they shrug,
pull random vials from shelves,
and fill a syringe to quiet and ease.

"No problem. How about a barrier here,
a sea wall here, or some extra sand?
Could we remodel ocean islands,
and plant tall grass to block waves?
In Holland they've coped for years,
so we can surely mitigate the effects
of storms like these."

There was of course no TV analysis
of what can exacerbate our illness–
what might accelerate methane flares
or spread extreme heat.

When a tumor is found in lung,
good doctors rail against smoking
even as they cut. But here,
earth will be fitted with straws
to bail swill. Gas, oil and coal firms
will drill mine burn
while pumps suck up flood.
Thus, *worse* will persist.

The Ocean's Illness

2015

"True, I was never calm.
Winds roiled me, cross currents
clashed within my swirls.
But now I'm forced to gulp
toxic beads, plastic waste,
and gas that brings heat down
from molten air and plumps
my drops with noxious froth.

"So acid now I can't bear more
(as I've swallowed junk for forty years),
my swelling seeps beneath the deepest
plunge of glacier to erase mass.
I clear out ice, I melt glassy weight.
Thawed methane below soon will spread.

"Bloated, ill, my heated body must
expand, and thus invade new space –
raise seas, flood streams, break walls,
soak streets. I flop and furl. Bouts
of shaking, epileptic fits
of vaulting waves are whipped
by wind, until I can't
control, can't even know

     where, or when,
        or what I'll fill –
            or how I'll flow."

Oxygen's Gavotte

2015

"A jolly element, fat
and inherently friendly,
eager to shake hands, clap backs,
join, I was for eons

"absent from the atmosphere
of an earth in back then rich in nitrogen,
methane, CO_2. Any small drop of myself
at the start would merge with iron-filled
rock to make an orange rust.

"Then came water-soaked microbes
that ate CO_2, and I was spewed as waste.
Oh happy day! Created as afterthought,
a prize not focused on, I was ignored.
But this hot, volcanic home was not
the place for me to gather strength.
I had to wait. When earth cooled,

I seized my chance. Attached to rock,
my rich breath let plants grow.
Microbes swelled as creatures
evolved to gulp me gladly, their lungs
and blood grateful pumps.

"I have since danced on a cosmic swing.
Up I go when carbon is stored
in woody plants. When trees exhale,
I fill the happy sky with life and ease.

*

"But if trees are hewn, and deserts grow,
I fall. Who then will make
O2 to breathe? Take heed,
for without me, your careless
species could simply…cease."

Water's Warning

"As only 5 % of me is fit
 to drink, I have been treasured.
Stored in Sumaria, piped through
Athens and aqueducts in Rome,
I was 'center of cities' in Angkor Wat,
and prized by Mayans.

"For only when my access is assured
can humans thrive. So the wise
make certain my route is safe.
Long ago, New York bought Catskill
watersheds, and lay pipes
so a billion gallons a day flow south –
a plan to be praised.

"Yet much of me is wasted daily.
183 gallons are sucked to grow
a pound of beef. Populations
swell, droughts drain aquifers
dry, and the up-draw of oil
and gas through long tubes
so humans can frack,
guzzles me mightily.
Pipes leak, waste is spewn,
till Love Canal, Flint, others
ruined beyond redeeming.

"And this on an earth where
I'm needed by all. Please
know and take heed. Thirst
is a gnawing curse
no one outgrows."

Earth's Words

Come off it! I've known mass extinctions
five times. You greedy creatures who complain
about this sixth simply wouldn't heed 'limits.'

I lost my *Gaptolites* 440 million years ago,
and later, my dear *Trilobites*, through no fault
of their own. They had sweet spiky armor
and multifaceted eyes. Come gas, flame, acid
and heat, most creatures vanished. That empty
Permian Age was tragic. In time, there was an eel-like
vertebrate, and then those audacious dinosaurs,
who reigned until their sudden *Cretaceous* death.

I do admit, as a mother, I'm uneasy
near the doorstep of your demise.
But don't spill tears. If you won't change,
simply mourning is a waste. Just hear me:
Once erased, your kind won't
be replaced. Some life will emerge,
but a species, once extinct, is not reborn.
Life-forms thrive, then rot.
For Sapiens, I doubt there'll be a second shot.

The Sun's Promise

"I am here – your helpmate and bride.
Occasional sun spots spike my touch, and ash
can dim my reach, but these are momentary blips
in an otherwise even flow of caring.
And now I see a race between those humans
eager to embrace new cells that capture and change
my force into usable power – and those still playing
with coal-oil-gas, most for personal gain.

"Imagine me among you as *a train*.
I hold work by chemists, physicists, designers
of cells—'thin film, micro-morphic, photovoltaic,
Titania, Perovskrite, poly-crytalines, Polyanilines,
polymers'—I count 200 books with myriad ways
to embrace my love. And there is new desire for

"*local* sharing, possible as the 'blockchain'
creates a ledger that tracks electrical generation,
path of travel, and end use – a secure, local
"transactive energy" record. This means
small players democratically involved.

"I try to pull uphill, but my body is weighed down
by frack beds, oil rigs, coal tar, nuke-waste –
all attached to my end. Meanwhile, my engine,
its solar tiles like diamonds on my roof, glides
on ray-capturing tracks. It hums that old
"think I can" tune. This is a titanic struggle,
a desperate race. Will they overwhelm me?
Pull me from the rail-bed entirely?
Will they crack my rear? But as the crest nears,

I pray markets will revolt and the old fall away
so I can exult. 'Ha! Thought I could,' I'll say.

"Then I would be fully yours, able to embrace you
closely, a soul-mate responsive to your needs
without investor money mangling romance.
I'd work with my friend, the oft-volatile wind.
You would feel our love as flowing light and heat
transmuted at your will and for your service.
Our union would birth an order that need not
exploit to reward. Indeed, our breath and beams,
if optimally used, would bring
                    a wondrous peace."

The Red Planet

"I was jealous from the start.
Not at first, when she was crusty as I.
But when she bloomed – a puberty
that led one-celled microbes (if soaked
wet) to birth myriad creatures that vaulted
toward life – Ah! Then! Her vaginal surface
opened to the rubbing of the sky against her flesh,
as she absorbed, conceived, and birthed
a trillion beings.
                                    "I was left out.
Wizened, cold, my water frozen beneath red rind,
I bore nothing alive. It was so for eons, I powerless
to change my orbit/ garner warmth and invite life,
although I tried. But now, it seems that

"much of my sister Earth dies! One rogue species
within her wealth proliferates wildly, and destroys.
Her coral reefs were killed by excess CO_2.
Her oceans acidic, those fish I'd watch
with longing now suffer and sink. Her Arctic ice
is so pitifully thin it cracks, melts and raises seas
that submerge coasts. And those dark forests,
glorious hair that adorned her body, seem pitifully
scant, through wanton cutting or lethal insects
brought by warming onto trees which can't, you know,
just pull up roots and move away. Much glorious
wildlife – so many colors, shapes, ways to feed,
play, fight, mate – now disappears.

"It won't be long before poor sister Earth
is barren as I. I'm predicting a grey surface –
a drab mix of sand and sticky clay.

"They say that NASA now has rockets to carry
a sapien-craft straight out to my space.
Maybe they deduce a blistering Earth
won't sustain them. Fine! There's nothing
they can ruin within me. I can't do much
to make them feel at home, but, please
let them know I eagerly wait. At last,
some absorbing variety. Some vibrant
life. So glad I'll no longer be alone."

Our Job Now

We are hurtling toward a cliff
too long unheeded. Not

       starved children, mothers
       in rags, folded on sand,
       soil, stone, weeping – no.

       Not hacked bodies, souls
       caught on the wrong side
       of danger, wrenched flesh adrift.

No. More steep. Rarely featured on TV,
barked at the fair for the mob,
or preached, most are still deaf
to a dim clock's tick.

       The scientist studying the melt
       of the Greenland shelf knows,
       but his voice's still no match
       for the market's throb.

It will not be easy to draw
the cliff on maps, illumine
the clock, or amplify its beat
to thunderous roar. But that

is our job.

A Kid Thinks About The Paris Conference - 2015

With thanks again to George Monbiot

"I think it's sorta like being really fat,
and you know you gotta lose weight
but still you eat your 6 Big Macs a day,
and that whole chocolate cake.
Then you add a salad – like that's gonna do it,
cause you didn't put no dressing on it
or anything that would, you know, add.

"So, are you gonna lose? Let's be real.
You gotta just stop pigging out, right? Just quit,
like, cold, and have maybe one Mac without
no bread and 6 salads, no cake, like that.

"So if it's hot here, an getting hotter,
an the heat is caused by trapped CO_2,
we've got to just quit makin' the stuff, man,
cause just addin' a bit of solar to the mix
ain't gonna do nothing. We gotta
keep that carbon deep down in the ground.

"But so what's our government doin?
A bit a' salad and a ton of Big Mac is what.
They're payin' billions every year
to companies that pull that black stuff up –
then sell it for burning. Why? So them
companies'll pay ta get 'em elected again.
But that bribe money'll make us sick –
drown us, burn us, rob us of water to drink,
an' get us all up an rollin on the road, searchin'
for any safe place, please God, just a good place to live!

"Meanwhile, all those guys on that stage
hugging, shaking hands, kissing, big grins
on their mugs, they didn't even say one word
'bout a binding law to keep those carbons
deep-sixed. Nothin' 'bout a tax. They're way happy
they've got a pledge that lets 'em just be dreamers,
or maybe traitors who've signed warrants for our death.
Pats on the back all round! 'Let's go,' they say.
"My treat. We'll pig out on Big Macs!"

God's Sorrow

"I had high hopes
as first I watched them.
Despite their childish grasping,
teenaged tantrums, spurts of vengeance,
I thought good sense could finally
lead them, squeeze them toward
Earth's redolent knock –
that shimmering joy
reached through sanity's waking.

"But now, not much I can do.
Evolution is law, and so
I've merely observed this species
throughout its loud, inventive rise,
even I surprised both by beauty
they'd create, and a vicious wrath
spewed while invoking my name.

"Well, let happen what must.
They battle without pause,
as though war could justify
cost, and ignore all warning.
And I can only mourn rising
seas and bombs shredding life.
In fact, current news renders cries
of their beleaguered sphere, mute –
for now the suicide belt as focus
eclipses a constant glacial drip.

"Unfair that my other species
will be caught too, diced
in drill bits, frack pipes,
poisoned by waste. But, no use

bewailing it. The whole is
too big for them to see.
Of course I'm depressed.
I am the force pulsing through
all life, yet I don't intervene
specifically – and so will
watch them fail,

"unless. . ."

CREDITS

"Attachments," *The Long Islander*, Huntington, Long
        Island, 2011.
"Song to the Earth: Sweat Lodge," *Naugatuck River
        Review*, November 2012.
"May 2009," *Chronogram*, June 2013.
"Albatross in the Midway Atoll," *Pacific Poetry Blog*, May
        2014.
"Late May," *The Kerf*, Fall, 2016.

WITH THANKS

To Charles Holdefer, for this kind nurturance and solid
poetic advice. To friends and members of writing groups
who helped with specific poems: Michelle Kagan, the late
David Kagan, Alan Iselin, Ted Strickroth, Van and Sandra
Howell, Alice Elman, Judith Ahrens, Douglas Kramer, Adele
Glimm, Myriam Chapman. To Jennifer Wilmshurst, my
cover co-conspirator, and to Jerri Bourrous of SFA Press,
who patiently and artistically transmuted my work into this
book. Finally, to my own dear partner Dan Maciejak, who
held me tightly through uncertainty.

AFTERWORD

Each of these poems was a reaction to disturbing news about climate change. Some were written in my own voice, but then I began to imagine what key players in our global drama might say. What words would the melting glacier utter? How would jellyfish react to their new dominion? Might CO2 apologize for its dreadful impact,and the rainforest eagerly offer us salvation? I heard many speeches – the sun, water, oxygen, suffering earth, ocean, our capitalist economy . . . Perhaps fittingly, God spoke last.

Packed with thorny "inconvenient truths," the book also references our two climate conferences (2009 and 2015), loci of both hope and disappointment. But much has changed since I began this work. Denial seemed endemic eight years ago, and, as with Cassandra, climate change was a hard sell. Now, bizarre weather often devastates. Even though some still cling to denial, debate is often front page news. Indeed, a brutal assessment of our situation by David Wallace Wells entitled "The Uninhabitable Earth" was just published in *New York Magazine*, July 10-23, 2017. His analysis offers a comprehensive picture of the destruction of Earth as habitation for our species.

We live in perilous times. It is difficult to know how to act, to react, to help. These poems document views from my window. As in the old folk song, I've tried to 'hammer out danger, to hammer out a warning.' We have a sacred home here on earth. It is my deep hope that we pay it careful attention, and are ultimately able to preserve both it – and ourselves.

ABOUT THE COVER

The cover photo is by James Balog, who has documented melting glaciers since the mid-80s. In 2007, he founded the Extreme Ice Survey (EIS), a project that merges art and science to give a "visual voice" to the planet's changing ecosystem. EIS installed time-lapse cameras at remote sites in Greenland, Iceland, Nepal, Alaska, and Antarctica. A new book, ICE: Portraits of Vanishing Glaciers (Rizzoli International), was released in September 2012 (www.jamesbalog.com).The cover photo depicts "icebergs which have calved from Jakobshavn Glacier as they float out to the sea near Ilulissat, Greenland. This glacier dumps more ice into the global ocean than any other in the Northern hemisphere, and is thus Greenland's single biggest contributor to the global sea level rise" (*Chasing Ice*, 2007).

In early July 2017, a billion-ton chunk of Antarctic ice shelf the size of Delaware broke away to float in the sea. Cracks have appeared along parts of the remaining shelf, and are expected to eventually shear off, as well. But, as Mr. Wallace Wells points out, calving icebergs and attendant sea level rise, though dramatic, is just one part of the complex situation we now face on Earth.

CPSIA information can be obtained
at www.ICGtesting.com
Printed in the USA
LVOW12s0327211017
553210LV00001BA/1/P

9 781622 881543